Is It Alive?

I0808866

Paul Gerber

INFOMAX COMMON CORE READERS

Rosen Classroom™

New York

Published in 2013 by The Rosen Publishing Group, Inc.
29 East 21st Street, New York, NY 10010

Book Design: Katelyn Londino

Photo Credits: Cover InavanHateren/Shutterstock.com; p. 4 Andrew Wakeford/Photodisc/Getty Images; p. 5 (watering can) DUSAN ZIDAR/Shutterstock.com; p. 5 (woman) Yuri Arcurs/Shutterstock.com; pp. 6, 15, 16 (grass) Dudarev Mikhail/Shutterstock.com; pp. 7, 16 (rain) © iStockphoto.com/kompasstudio; pp. 7, 16 (sunlight) vovan/Shutterstock.com; p. 8 Fotosearch/Fotosearch/Getty Images; pp. 9, 15 (ball) Iakov Filimonov/Shutterstock.com; pp. 10, 15 (cow) aleks.k/Shutterstock.com; p. 11 Dudarev Mikhail/Shutterstock.com; p. 12 © iStockphoto.com/gilmourbto2001; pp. 13, 15 (rock) schankz/Shutterstock.com; p. 14 © iStockphoto.com/kali9.

ISBN: 978-1-4488-8965-5
6-pack ISBN: 978-1-4488-8966-2

Manufactured in the United States of America

CPSIA Compliance Information: Batch #WS12RC: For further information contact Rosen Publishing, New York, New York at 1-800-237-9932.

Word Count: 100

Contents

Living things are alive.

Nonliving things are not alive.

Living things need food and water to stay alive.

Is a tree alive?

Yes, a tree is alive.

It gets water from the rain.

It uses sunlight to make food.

Is a ball alive?

No, a ball is not alive.

A ball doesn't need food and water.

Is a cow alive?

Yes, a cow is alive.

It eats grass and drinks water.

Is a rock alive?

No, a rock is not alive.

A rock doesn't need food and water.

Look all around you.

Can you name other things that are alive?